EMMANUEL JOSEPH

The New World Builders, How Billionaires Are Reshaping Countries and Their Futures

Copyright © 2025 by Emmanuel Joseph

All rights reserved. No part of this publication may be reproduced, stored or transmitted in any form or by any means, electronic, mechanical, photocopying, recording, scanning, or otherwise without written permission from the publisher. It is illegal to copy this book, post it to a website, or distribute it by any other means without permission.

First edition

This book was professionally typeset on Reedsy.
Find out more at reedsy.com

Contents

1	Chapter 1: The Rise of the Modern Billionaire	1
2	Chapter 2: The Tech Titans	3
3	Chapter 3: The Philanthropic Visionaries	5
4	Chapter 4: The Energy Pioneers	7
5	Chapter 5: The Media Moguls	9
6	Chapter 6: The Real Estate Magnates	11
7	Chapter 7: The Financial Titans	13
8	Chapter 8: The Healthcare Innovators	15
9	Chapter 9: The Cultural Patrons	17
10	Chapter 10: The Education Advocates	19
11	Chapter 11: The Environmental Stewards	21
12	Chapter 12: The Social Entrepreneurs	23
13	Chapter 13: The Political Influencers	25
14	Chapter 14: The Sports Moguls	27
15	Chapter 15: The Fashion Icons	29
16	Chapter 16: The Space Explorers	31
17	Chapter 17: The Future Builders	33

1

Chapter 1: The Rise of the Modern Billionaire

In the 21st century, the concept of wealth has transcended traditional boundaries, and billionaires have become the new architects of global change. With vast resources at their disposal, these individuals wield unprecedented influence over economies, politics, and societal norms. The rise of the modern billionaire is not just a story of financial success; it is a tale of ambition, vision, and a relentless drive to reshape the world according to their ideals. From Silicon Valley tech giants to oil magnates in the Middle East, these new world builders are redefining what it means to have power and control in the contemporary era.

The influence of billionaires extends far beyond their business ventures. Through philanthropic endeavors, they are tackling some of the world's most pressing issues, from climate change to poverty eradication. Foundations established by figures like Bill Gates and Warren Buffett are channeling billions of dollars into scientific research, education, and healthcare. These initiatives are not just acts of charity; they are strategic investments aimed at creating a sustainable and equitable future. By leveraging their wealth for the greater good, billionaires are positioning themselves as pivotal players in the quest for global progress.

However, the growing power of billionaires also raises critical questions about inequality and democracy. The concentration of wealth in the hands of a few has led to a widening gap between the rich and the poor, exacerbating social tensions and fueling populist movements. Critics argue that the influence of billionaires undermines democratic institutions, as they can shape public policy and elections through their financial contributions. This dynamic has sparked debates about the need for regulatory measures to ensure a more balanced distribution of power and resources.

Ultimately, the rise of the modern billionaire represents a paradigm shift in the global landscape. These individuals are not just passive beneficiaries of wealth; they are active agents of change with the potential to reshape the future. As we move further into the 21st century, the role of billionaires in society will continue to evolve, and their actions will undoubtedly leave an indelible mark on the world stage.

2

Chapter 2: The Tech Titans

In the digital age, tech billionaires have emerged as some of the most influential figures in the world. Visionaries like Elon Musk, Jeff Bezos, and Mark Zuckerberg have not only revolutionized industries but have also profoundly impacted our daily lives. Their companies, such as Tesla, Amazon, and Facebook, have become integral parts of the global economy, driving innovation and shaping consumer behavior. The reach of these tech giants extends far beyond their core businesses, as they invest in cutting-edge technologies, space exploration, and artificial intelligence, envisioning a future that was once the realm of science fiction.

The transformative power of technology has given these billionaires a unique platform to address global challenges. Elon Musk's SpaceX aims to make space travel more accessible, with the ultimate goal of colonizing Mars. Jeff Bezos' Blue Origin also seeks to pave the way for humanity's expansion into space. Meanwhile, Mark Zuckerberg's philanthropic efforts focus on advancing internet connectivity and education. These initiatives reflect a broader trend among tech billionaires: using their wealth and expertise to push the boundaries of what is possible and drive progress on a global scale.

However, the dominance of tech billionaires also raises ethical and regulatory concerns. The immense power concentrated in the hands of a few has led to debates about data privacy, market monopolies, and the societal impact of automation. Critics argue that the unchecked influence of these tech giants can stifle competition and undermine democratic processes. As governments grapple with these challenges, the need for comprehensive regulations to ensure a fair and equitable digital landscape becomes increasingly apparent.

Despite the controversies, the contributions of tech billionaires to technological advancement and societal progress cannot be ignored. Their vision and ambition have propelled humanity into a new era of innovation, reshaping the way we live, work, and interact. As we navigate the complexities of the digital age, the role of tech titans in shaping our future will continue to be a subject of fascination and scrutiny.

3

Chapter 3: The Philanthropic Visionaries

Philanthropy has become a defining characteristic of the modern billionaire, with many of the world's wealthiest individuals dedicating substantial portions of their fortunes to charitable causes. The philanthropic efforts of billionaires like Bill Gates, Warren Buffett, and Oprah Winfrey have had a profound impact on global issues such as healthcare, education, and poverty alleviation. Through their foundations and personal initiatives, these visionaries are addressing some of the world's most pressing challenges, demonstrating that wealth can be a powerful force for good.

Bill Gates, co-founder of Microsoft, has become one of the most prominent figures in global philanthropy. The Bill & Melinda Gates Foundation, established in 2000, has invested billions of dollars in initiatives aimed at improving healthcare, reducing extreme poverty, and expanding educational opportunities. Gates' focus on eradicating diseases such as malaria and polio has led to significant advancements in medical research and public health. His commitment to philanthropy has inspired other billionaires to follow suit, creating a ripple effect of positive change.

Warren Buffett, one of the most successful investors in history, has also made a significant impact through his philanthropic endeavors. In 2006, Buffett pledged to give away the majority of his fortune to charitable causes, primarily through the Gates Foundation. His approach to philanthropy emphasizes strategic investments and collaboration, with the goal of maximizing the effectiveness of charitable efforts. Buffett's generosity and pragmatic approach have set a new standard for billionaire philanthropy, encouraging others to contribute their wealth to address societal challenges.

Oprah Winfrey, a media mogul and cultural icon, has used her platform and resources to empower and uplift marginalized communities. Through the Oprah Winfrey Foundation and the Oprah Winfrey Leadership Academy for Girls, she has focused on education and empowerment, particularly for young women in Africa. Winfrey's philanthropic efforts reflect her commitment to creating opportunities and fostering positive change, demonstrating the transformative potential of wealth when guided by compassion and vision.

The rise of philanthropic billionaires represents a shift in how wealth is perceived and utilized. Rather than merely accumulating riches, these individuals are leveraging their resources to make a meaningful difference in the world. Their contributions have the potential to drive progress on a global scale, addressing systemic issues and creating a more equitable and sustainable future.

4

Chapter 4: The Energy Pioneers

In the quest for a sustainable future, billionaires in the energy sector have emerged as key players. Innovators like Elon Musk, Richard Branson, and Bill Gates are investing heavily in renewable energy technologies, seeking to reduce our reliance on fossil fuels and mitigate the impacts of climate change. Their efforts are transforming the energy landscape and shaping the future of global energy production.

Elon Musk's Tesla has revolutionized the electric vehicle industry, making electric cars more accessible and desirable. Tesla's advancements in battery technology and renewable energy storage have also paved the way for more efficient and sustainable energy solutions. Musk's vision for a future powered by clean energy extends beyond electric vehicles, as Tesla's solar products and energy storage systems are designed to reduce dependence on traditional power grids.

Richard Branson's Virgin Group has also made significant strides in the renewable energy sector. Through Virgin Galactic, Branson aims to develop sustainable space travel, while Virgin Green Fund invests in innovative clean energy technologies. Branson's commitment to sustainability is evident in his various ventures, which prioritize environmental responsibility and aim to create a greener future for all.

Bill Gates, through his Breakthrough Energy Ventures, is investing in cutting-edge technologies that have the potential to revolutionize energy production and consumption. From advanced nuclear reactors to carbon capture and storage solutions, Gates is supporting a wide range of initiatives that seek to address the world's energy challenges. His philanthropic efforts also focus on promoting sustainable agricultural practices and improving energy access in developing countries, highlighting the interconnectedness of energy, food security, and economic development.

The contributions of these energy pioneers are driving the transition to a more sustainable and resilient energy system. Their investments and innovations are not only helping to combat climate change but also creating new economic opportunities and fostering technological advancements. As the world grapples with the urgent need for sustainable solutions, the role of billionaires in the energy sector will continue to be critical in shaping our collective future.

5

Chapter 5: The Media Moguls

The media landscape has been profoundly shaped by billionaires who control major news outlets, entertainment companies, and social media platforms. Figures like Rupert Murdoch, Ted Turner, and Shonda Rhimes have wielded their influence to shape public discourse, culture, and political narratives. The media moguls of the modern era are not just content creators; they are powerful gatekeepers who determine what information reaches the masses and how it is presented.

Rupert Murdoch, the founder of News Corporation, has built a global media empire that spans newspapers, television networks, and digital platforms. His influence on public opinion and political affairs is unparalleled, as his media outlets have the power to shape narratives and sway elections. Murdoch's ability to leverage his media assets for political and economic gain has made him one of the most powerful and controversial figures in the industry.

Ted Turner, the founder of CNN, revolutionized the way news is delivered and consumed. As the pioneer of 24-hour news, Turner transformed the media landscape by providing real-time coverage of global events. His contributions to journalism and media have had a lasting impact on how news is reported and disseminated, setting new standards for the industry. Turner's philanthropic efforts, including his substantial donations to environmental causes, reflect his commitment to using his wealth for positive change.

Shonda Rhimes, a trailblazing television producer and writer, has reshaped the entertainment industry with her groundbreaking work on shows like "Grey's Anatomy" and "Scandal." Rhimes' influence extends beyond her creative achievements, as she has championed diversity and inclusion in Hollywood. Through her production company, Shondaland, Rhimes is creating opportunities for underrepresented voices and challenging the industry's status quo. Her impact on popular culture and storytelling is a testament to the power of media moguls in shaping societal norms and values.

The influence of media moguls on public perception and cultural trends cannot be overstated. Their control over information and entertainment gives them significant power to shape opinions and drive societal change. As the media landscape continues to evolve, the role of these billionaires in shaping our collective consciousness will remain a critical aspect of their legacy.

6

Chapter 6: The Real Estate Magnates

Real estate billionaires have played a crucial role in shaping urban landscapes and influencing economic development. Visionaries like Donald Trump, Li Ka-shing, and Jorge Pérez have transformed cities through their ambitious projects, creating iconic skylines and revitalizing communities. The impact of real estate magnates on urban planning, architecture, and the housing market is profound, as they navigate the complexities of property development and investment.

Donald Trump, before his presidency, made a name for himself as a real estate mogul with his luxury hotels, residential towers, and golf courses. Trump's brand became synonymous with opulence and success, attracting high-profile tenants and investors. His real estate ventures not only shaped the skylines of major cities but also influenced the industry's standards for luxury and exclusivity. Trump's ability to leverage his real estate assets for political and business purposes exemplifies the intersection of wealth, power, and influence.

Li Ka-shing, one of Asia's richest individuals, has built a vast real estate empire through his companies Cheung Kong Holdings and Hutchison Whampoa. His developments in Hong Kong and mainland China have had a significant impact on urbanization and economic growth in the region. Li's investments in infrastructure, telecommunications, and energy further illustrate his diverse business interests and strategic vision. His philanthropic contributions to education and healthcare reflect his commitment to giving back to society and improving the quality of life for future generations.

Jorge Pérez, known as the "Condo King," has transformed Miami's skyline with his luxury condominium developments. As the founder of Related Group, Pérez has played a pivotal role in the revitalization of urban areas and the creation of vibrant communities. His focus on sustainable development and affordable housing demonstrates his commitment to addressing the diverse needs of urban populations. Pérez's contributions to the arts and culture further highlight his dedication to enhancing the social fabric of the cities he helps shape.

The influence of real estate magnates on urban development and economic prosperity is undeniable. Their visionary projects and strategic investments have the power to transform cities and improve the quality of life for residents. As urbanization continues to accelerate, the role of real estate billionaires in shaping the future of our cities will remain a critical aspect of their legacy.

7

Chapter 7: The Financial Titans

Financial billionaires have long been the backbone of the global economy, shaping markets and influencing economic policies. Figures like Warren Buffett, George Soros, and Ray Dalio have amassed fortunes through their mastery of investing, hedge funds, and asset management. Their strategies and decisions have far-reaching implications, impacting everything from stock prices to monetary policies.

Warren Buffett, known as the "Oracle of Omaha," has built his wealth through his investment firm, Berkshire Hathaway. Buffett's value investing approach, which focuses on identifying undervalued companies with strong fundamentals, has earned him a reputation as one of the greatest investors of all time. His annual letters to shareholders are widely read and respected, offering insights into his investment philosophy and market outlook. Beyond his financial success, Buffett's commitment to philanthropy, including his pledge to give away the majority of his fortune, sets him apart as a financial titan with a moral compass.

George Soros, founder of Soros Fund Management, is another influential figure in the world of finance. Soros is known for his bold investment strategies and willingness to take significant risks, including his famous bet against the British pound in 1992, which earned him over a billion dollars in a single day. Soros' success in the financial markets has allowed him to become a prominent philanthropist and political activist. Through his Open

Society Foundations, he supports initiatives that promote democracy, human rights, and social justice around the world.

Ray Dalio, the founder of Bridgewater Associates, has revolutionized the hedge fund industry with his unique approach to investing. Dalio's emphasis on principles-based decision-making and radical transparency has set Bridgewater apart as one of the most successful and innovative hedge funds. Dalio's principles, outlined in his bestselling book, have resonated with investors and business leaders, offering a framework for achieving success in both personal and professional endeavors. His philanthropic efforts, including support for education and environmental causes, reflect his commitment to making a positive impact beyond the financial world.

The influence of financial titans extends far beyond their investment portfolios. Their insights and strategies shape market trends, while their philanthropic contributions address pressing global challenges. As the financial landscape continues to evolve, the role of these billionaires in shaping economic policies and driving social change will remain a critical aspect of their legacy.

8

Chapter 8: The Healthcare Innovators

In the realm of healthcare, billionaires have emerged as key players in driving medical advancements and improving global health outcomes. Visionaries like Patrick Soon-Shiong, Larry Ellison, and Priscilla Chan are leveraging their wealth and expertise to tackle some of the most challenging health issues of our time. Their contributions to medical research, biotechnology, and healthcare access are transforming the industry and shaping the future of medicine.

Patrick Soon-Shiong, a surgeon and entrepreneur, is known for his pioneering work in cancer treatment and biotechnology. Through his company, NantWorks, Soon-Shiong is developing innovative therapies and diagnostics aimed at personalized medicine. His efforts to advance cancer research and improve patient outcomes have earned him recognition as one of the most influential figures in healthcare. Soon-Shiong's philanthropic initiatives, including support for medical research and healthcare access in underserved communities, reflect his commitment to making a difference in the lives of patients around the world.

Larry Ellison, co-founder of Oracle, has also made significant contributions to healthcare through his philanthropic endeavors. The Larry Ellison Foundation supports initiatives focused on global health, infectious disease research, and healthcare innovation. Ellison's investments in biotechnology and life sciences are aimed at addressing some of the most pressing health challenges, including aging and chronic diseases. His commitment to advancing medical research and improving healthcare outcomes underscores the potential of billionaires to drive meaningful change in the industry.

Priscilla Chan, a pediatrician and philanthropist, along with her husband Mark Zuckerberg, has established the Chan Zuckerberg Initiative (CZI) to support scientific research and healthcare innovation. CZI's ambitious goal of curing, preventing, or managing all diseases by the end of the century reflects the scale of their vision and commitment. Through investments in scientific research, education, and community health programs, Chan is leveraging her medical background to address health disparities and promote wellness on a global scale.

The contributions of healthcare innovators are reshaping the industry and improving the quality of life for millions of people. Their investments in research, technology, and healthcare access are driving progress and creating new opportunities for medical breakthroughs. As the world continues to face health challenges, the role of these billionaires in advancing healthcare and shaping the future of medicine will remain a critical aspect of their legacy.

9

Chapter 9: The Cultural Patrons

Billionaires have long played a significant role in supporting the arts and culture, using their wealth to preserve heritage, promote artistic expression, and foster creativity. Philanthropists like David Geffen, Alice Walton, and François Pinault have made substantial contributions to museums, performing arts centers, and cultural institutions, ensuring that the arts continue to thrive and inspire future generations.

David Geffen, a music and film mogul, has been a prominent supporter of the arts for decades. His generous donations to institutions like the Museum of Modern Art, the Los Angeles County Museum of Art, and Lincoln Center have helped fund exhibitions, educational programs, and renovations. Geffen's commitment to the arts extends beyond financial support, as he has also played a role in shaping cultural initiatives and promoting artistic innovation.

Alice Walton, an heir to the Walmart fortune, has made significant contributions to the arts through her establishment of the Crystal Bridges Museum of American Art in Arkansas. The museum, which houses an impressive collection of American art, aims to make art accessible to a broad audience and foster a deeper appreciation for the nation's cultural heritage. Walton's philanthropy reflects her passion for the arts and her dedication to enriching the cultural landscape of her community.

François Pinault, a French luxury goods magnate, has amassed one of the world's most extensive contemporary art collections. His commitment to the arts is evident in his establishment of the Pinault Collection, which includes works by renowned artists such as Jeff Koons, Damien Hirst, and Cindy Sherman. Pinault's contributions to the arts extend beyond his collection, as he has also funded the restoration of historic buildings and supported cultural events and exhibitions.

The impact of cultural patrons on the arts and society is profound. Their support ensures that artistic expression continues to flourish, enriching our lives and shaping our understanding of the world. As the arts face challenges in an increasingly digital and commercialized landscape, the role of billionaire patrons in preserving and promoting culture will remain a vital aspect of their legacy.

10

Chapter 10: The Education Advocates

Education has long been seen as a powerful tool for change, and billionaires who champion educational causes are making significant strides in transforming the sector. Prominent figures like Bill Gates, Mark Zuckerberg, and Laurene Powell Jobs are investing in innovative educational initiatives and technologies, with the aim of providing quality education to underserved communities and preparing the next generation for the challenges of the future.

Bill Gates, through the Bill & Melinda Gates Foundation, has made substantial contributions to education reform. The foundation's initiatives focus on improving K-12 education, expanding access to higher education, and promoting innovation in teaching and learning. Gates' commitment to education is driven by his belief that a strong education system is essential for economic growth and social mobility. By investing in research, technology, and policy advocacy, Gates is working to create a more equitable and effective educational landscape.

Mark Zuckerberg, along with his wife Priscilla Chan, has also made significant investments in education through the Chan Zuckerberg Initiative (CZI). CZI's education programs aim to personalize learning, support teachers, and develop innovative educational tools and resources. The initiative's focus on equity and access reflects Zuckerberg and Chan's commitment to ensuring that all students, regardless of their background, have the opportunity to succeed. Their efforts to leverage technology for educational advancement are reshaping the way students learn and interact with information.

Laurene Powell Jobs, the widow of Apple co-founder Steve Jobs, has dedicated much of her philanthropic work to education through her organization, Emerson Collective. The organization supports a wide range of educational initiatives, from school reform to college access programs. Powell Jobs' approach emphasizes the importance of innovation, collaboration, and community involvement in addressing educational challenges. Her efforts to create systemic change in the education sector highlight the potential of philanthropic leadership to drive meaningful progress.

The contributions of education advocates are transforming the sector and creating new opportunities for learners around the world. Their investments in research, technology, and policy reform are addressing systemic issues and promoting a more inclusive and effective education system. As the world faces the challenges of the 21st century, the role of billionaire education advocates in shaping the future of learning will remain a critical aspect of their legacy.

11

Chapter 11: The Environmental Stewards

As the world grapples with the urgent need to address climate change and environmental degradation, billionaires who champion environmental causes are playing a pivotal role. Visionaries like Jeff Bezos, Leonardo DiCaprio, and Michael Bloomberg are leveraging their wealth and influence to promote sustainability, conservation, and environmental justice. Their efforts are not only raising awareness but also driving tangible action to protect the planet for future generations.

Jeff Bezos, the founder of Amazon, has made significant investments in environmental initiatives through the Bezos Earth Fund. The fund, which aims to allocate $10 billion to combat climate change, supports a wide range of projects focused on reducing carbon emissions, restoring ecosystems, and advancing renewable energy. Bezos' commitment to sustainability is also reflected in Amazon's pledge to achieve net-zero carbon emissions by 2040. His efforts to address environmental challenges underscore the potential of billionaire philanthropy to drive meaningful change.

Leonardo DiCaprio, an actor and environmental activist, has used his platform and resources to advocate for environmental conservation and climate action. Through the Leonardo DiCaprio Foundation, he has supported projects focused on protecting biodiversity, promoting renewable energy, and advocating for climate policy. DiCaprio's activism has brought attention to critical environmental issues and inspired others to take action.

His commitment to environmental stewardship reflects the power of celebrity influence in driving social and environmental change.

Michael Bloomberg, a former mayor of New York City and founder of Bloomberg LP, has been a leading advocate for environmental causes. Through his philanthropy, Bloomberg has supported initiatives focused on clean energy, climate resilience, and public health. His work with organizations like the C40 Cities Climate Leadership Group highlights the importance of collaboration and policy innovation in addressing climate change. Bloomberg's efforts to promote sustainability and environmental justice demonstrate the impact of billionaire leadership in advancing global environmental goals.

The contributions of environmental stewards are critical in the fight against climate change and environmental degradation. Their investments in research, conservation, and policy advocacy are driving progress and creating new opportunities for sustainable development. As the world faces the pressing challenges of the 21st century, the role of billionaire environmental advocates in shaping a more sustainable future will remain a vital aspect of their legacy.

12

Chapter 12: The Social Entrepreneurs

Social entrepreneurs are using their wealth and influence to address pressing social issues and create positive change in their communities. Billionaires like Pierre Omidyar, Richard Branson, and Sheryl Sandberg are leveraging their business acumen and resources to develop innovative solutions to social challenges. Their efforts are transforming industries and improving the lives of countless individuals around the world.

Pierre Omidyar, the founder of eBay, has dedicated much of his philanthropic work to social entrepreneurship through the Omidyar Network. The organization invests in social enterprises that aim to create positive social impact, from financial inclusion to education and governance. Omidyar's approach emphasizes the importance of market-based solutions and entrepreneurship in addressing systemic issues. His commitment to social entrepreneurship reflects his belief in the power of innovation and business to drive meaningful change.

Richard Branson, the founder of the Virgin Group, has also made significant contributions to social entrepreneurship through his various ventures and philanthropic initiatives. Branson's focus on sustainability, innovation, and social impact is evident in his support for organizations like Virgin Unite, which works to address issues such as climate change, education, and healthcare. Branson's entrepreneurial spirit and commitment to creating positive change demonstrate the potential of business leaders to make a difference in the world.

Sheryl Sandberg, the Chief Operating Officer of Facebook, has used her platform and resources to advocate for gender equality and women's empowerment. Through her Lean In initiative, Sandberg has inspired women around the world to pursue their ambitions and challenge societal norms. Her work to promote diversity and inclusion in the workplace reflects her commitment to creating a more equitable and just society. Sandberg's contributions to social entrepreneurship highlight the importance of leadership and advocacy in driving social change.

The contributions of social entrepreneurs are transforming industries and improving the quality of life for individuals around the world. Their investments in innovative solutions and their commitment to social impact are addressing critical challenges and creating new opportunities for progress. As the world faces complex social issues, the role of billionaire social entrepreneurs in shaping a more just and equitable future will remain a critical aspect of their legacy.

13

Chapter 13: The Political Influencers

Billionaires wield considerable influence in the political arena, shaping public policy and political discourse through their financial contributions and advocacy efforts. Figures like Michael Bloomberg, George Soros, and the Koch brothers have used their wealth to support political candidates, fund advocacy groups, and promote their policy agendas. Their involvement in politics raises important questions about the role of money in democracy and the impact of billionaire influence on the political process.

Michael Bloomberg, a former mayor of New York City and founder of Bloomberg LP, has been a prominent figure in American politics. His substantial financial contributions to political campaigns and advocacy organizations have made him a key player in shaping public policy. Bloomberg's support for issues such as gun control, climate change, and public health reflects his commitment to addressing pressing societal challenges. His involvement in politics underscores the power of billionaire influence in driving political change.

George Soros, founder of the Open Society Foundations, has been a significant force in promoting democracy, human rights, and social justice around the world. Soros' financial support for political candidates and advocacy groups has made him a polarizing figure, with critics arguing that his influence undermines democratic processes. Despite the controversies,

Soros' commitment to advancing democratic values and promoting social change reflects his belief in the power of philanthropy to shape a better world.

The Koch brothers, Charles and the late David Koch, have been influential figures in American politics through their support for conservative causes and candidates. Their extensive network of advocacy organizations and think tanks has shaped public policy on issues such as taxation, regulation, and free-market principles. The Koch brothers' involvement in politics highlights the complex and often contentious role of billionaire influence in shaping political discourse and policy outcomes.

The involvement of billionaires in politics raises important questions about the role of money in democracy and the impact of their influence on the political process. While their financial contributions and advocacy efforts can drive meaningful change, they also raise concerns about the concentration of power and the potential for undue influence. As the political landscape continues to evolve, the role of billionaire political influencers in shaping public policy and political discourse will remain a critical aspect of their legacy.

14

Chapter 14: The Sports Moguls

Billionaires have also made significant impacts in the world of sports, transforming teams, leagues, and the overall fan experience. Figures like Jerry Jones, Roman Abramovich, and Steve Ballmer have invested heavily in sports franchises, using their resources to build successful teams and enhance the entertainment value of sports. Their influence extends beyond the field, as they shape the business and cultural aspects of sports.

Jerry Jones, the owner of the Dallas Cowboys, has revolutionized the business of American football. Under his ownership, the Cowboys have become one of the most valuable sports franchises in the world. Jones' investments in state-of-the-art facilities, marketing, and branding have elevated the team's profile and set new standards for the industry. His influence on the NFL extends to his role in negotiating television contracts and league policies, making him one of the most powerful figures in American sports.

Roman Abramovich, the owner of Chelsea Football Club, has transformed the landscape of European soccer. Since acquiring the club in 2003, Abramovich has invested heavily in player acquisitions, facilities, and management, leading Chelsea to numerous domestic and international titles. His willingness to spend on top talent and infrastructure has set a precedent for other club owners, raising the level of competition and professionalism in the sport. Abramovich's impact on soccer extends beyond Chelsea, as his investments have contributed to the global growth and popularity of the game.

Steve Ballmer, the former CEO of Microsoft, has brought his business acumen and enthusiasm to the world of basketball as the owner of the Los Angeles Clippers. Ballmer's investments in the team and its facilities have revitalized the franchise and energized its fan base. His commitment to innovation and fan engagement is evident in his efforts to enhance the game-day experience and leverage technology to connect with supporters. Ballmer's influence on the NBA reflects the potential of billionaire ownership to drive positive change and elevate the sport.

The contributions of sports moguls are shaping the future of athletics and entertainment. Their investments in teams, facilities, and fan experiences are driving the evolution of sports as a global industry. As the world of sports continues to grow and evolve, the role of billionaire owners in shaping the business and cultural aspects of the industry will remain a critical aspect of their legacy.

15

Chapter 15: The Fashion Icons

In the world of fashion, billionaires have made significant contributions to the industry, shaping trends, and influencing consumer behavior. Visionaries like Bernard Arnault, Amancio Ortega, and Ralph Lauren have built iconic brands that define luxury, style, and innovation. Their influence extends beyond the runway, as they shape the business and cultural aspects of fashion.

Bernard Arnault, the chairman and CEO of LVMH, has built a luxury empire that includes brands like Louis Vuitton, Dior, and Givenchy. Arnault's strategic acquisitions and investments have made LVMH the world's largest luxury goods company. His influence on the fashion industry is unparalleled, as he shapes trends and sets standards for quality and innovation. Arnault's commitment to craftsmanship and creativity has elevated the perception of luxury and redefined the fashion landscape.

Amancio Ortega, the founder of Inditex, has revolutionized the fashion industry with his fast-fashion brand, Zara. Ortega's business model, which emphasizes rapid production and affordable prices, has made Zara one of the most successful and influential fashion retailers in the world. His approach to fashion democratizes style, making high-quality, trendy clothing accessible to a broad audience. Ortega's impact on the industry extends to his innovative supply chain and retail strategies, which have set new benchmarks for efficiency and customer satisfaction.

Ralph Lauren, an iconic American designer, has built a global brand that embodies timeless elegance and sophistication. Lauren's vision and creativity have made his eponymous brand synonymous with luxury and classic style. His influence on fashion extends beyond his designs, as he has shaped the industry's approach to branding, marketing, and lifestyle. Lauren's commitment to philanthropy and social responsibility further highlights his impact on the fashion world and society at large.

The contributions of fashion icons are shaping the future of the industry and influencing consumer behavior. Their investments in design, innovation, and branding are driving the evolution of fashion as a global business. As the fashion industry continues to grow and adapt to changing trends, the role of billionaire designers and entrepreneurs in shaping the business and cultural aspects of fashion will remain a critical aspect of their legacy.

16

Chapter 16: The Space Explorers

Billionaires are also playing a pivotal role in the new era of space exploration, pushing the boundaries of what is possible and paving the way for humanity's future in space. Visionaries like Elon Musk, Jeff Bezos, and Richard Branson are leading the charge with their ambitious space ventures, aiming to make space travel more accessible and sustainable.

Elon Musk's SpaceX has revolutionized the space industry with its reusable rockets and ambitious plans for interplanetary travel. Musk's vision of colonizing Mars and making humanity a multi-planetary species has captured the imagination of people around the world. SpaceX's achievements, including the successful launch and landing of the Falcon Heavy and the development of the Starship spacecraft, are setting new standards for space exploration and technology.

Jeff Bezos' Blue Origin is also making significant strides in space exploration, with a focus on building a sustainable future in space. Bezos' vision of millions of people living and working in space is driving the development of reusable rockets and advanced space habitats. Blue Origin's New Shepard and New Glenn rockets are designed to make space travel more affordable and accessible, paving the way for future generations to explore and utilize space resources.

Richard Branson's Virgin Galactic is pioneering commercial space tourism, offering suborbital flights to the edge of space. Branson's commitment to making space travel accessible to the public is reflected in his efforts to create a safe and enjoyable experience for passengers. Virgin Galactic's SpaceShipTwo has successfully completed test flights, bringing the dream of space tourism closer to reality. Branson's vision of democratizing space travel is inspiring a new generation of space enthusiasts and adventurers.

The contributions of space explorers are driving the next frontier of human exploration and innovation. Their investments in technology, infrastructure, and research are opening new possibilities for space travel and utilization. As humanity looks to the stars, the role of billionaire space pioneers in shaping the future of space exploration will remain a critical aspect of their legacy.

17

Chapter 17: The Future Builders

As we look to the future, billionaires will continue to play a pivotal role in shaping the world and addressing the challenges of the 21st century. Their wealth, influence, and vision position them as key players in driving innovation, progress, and social change. The future builders of tomorrow will leverage their resources to tackle pressing global issues, from climate change to inequality, and create a more sustainable and equitable world.

The next generation of billionaires will build on the foundations laid by their predecessors, using their wealth and expertise to drive progress in fields such as technology, healthcare, education, and the environment. Their commitment to philanthropy and social impact will continue to inspire positive change and create new opportunities for growth and development.

As the world becomes increasingly interconnected and complex, the role of billionaires in shaping the future will be more important than ever. Their ability to influence public policy, drive technological advancements, and address global challenges will be critical in creating a better world for future generations. The legacy of the new world builders will be defined by their contributions to society and their efforts to create a more just, sustainable, and prosperous future.

Book Description:
In a world where wealth translates to power and influence, "The New

World Builders" delves into the profound impact billionaires are having on our global landscape. This captivating exploration sheds light on how these modern titans are not just amassing fortunes but are actively shaping the future of countries and societies.

From the trailblazing tech giants who are revolutionizing industries and daily lives, to the philanthropic visionaries dedicating their riches to solving global crises, this book provides a comprehensive look at the diverse ways in which billionaires are driving change. It highlights the efforts of energy pioneers transforming our approach to sustainability, media moguls controlling the narrative, and healthcare innovators pushing the boundaries of medical science.

Discover the stories of financial titans who move markets and influence economic policies, real estate magnates who shape urban landscapes, and cultural patrons preserving heritage and fostering creativity. Explore the ambitious ventures of space explorers, the transformative power of social entrepreneurs, and the critical role of political influencers in shaping public policy.

"The New World Builders" also addresses the ethical and regulatory challenges posed by the concentration of wealth and power, sparking essential debates about democracy and inequality. As we navigate the complexities of the 21st century, this book offers a thought-provoking analysis of the roles and responsibilities of the world's wealthiest individuals.

Join us on a journey through the lives and legacies of the billionaires who are reshaping our world and our future. This book is a testament to the extraordinary influence of wealth and the enduring quest for progress and innovation.

www.ingramcontent.com/pod-product-compliance
Lightning Source LLC
LaVergne TN
LVHW010441070526
838199LV00066B/6137